Arletha Orr

All scripture quotations marked NKJV are taken from the New King James Version®. Copyright © 1982 by Thomas Nelson. Used by permission. All rights reserved.

All Scripture quotations marked MSG are taken from THE MESSAGE, copyright © 1993, 2002, 2018 by Eugene H. Peterson. Used by permission of NavPress, represented by Tyndale House Publishers. All rights reserved.

LIVE. Copyright © 2021 All rights reserved – Arletha Orr

No portion of this book may be reproduced or transmitted in any form or by any means, graphic, electronic, or mechanical, including photocopying, recording, taping, or by information storage retrieval system without the written permission of the publisher.

Please direct all copyright inquiries to:
Kingdom Trailblazers
c/o Author Copyrights
Post Office Box 767
Flora, MS 39071

Paperback ISBN: 978-1-7379781-0-7

Design: Kingdom Trailblazers Publishing

Printed in the United States.

I dedicate this book to Lil Michael, Mikilah & Michael…#teamAllen! You all will forever be in my heart. I love you!

I want to thank God, first and foremost, for allowing me to be able to Minister and help others overcome. I know and understand that He is sovereign, and everything happens for a reason. Secondly, thanks to my family for being with me every step of the way. Lastly, Author Lorieen for encouraging me and pushing me to move forward when I wanted to give up.

Table of Contents

The Plan 7

Who Am I 16

Sanctification & The Anointing 25

The Heartbreak 33

Broken but Healed 44

Resentment & Shock 54

Come out of Lo-debar 59

God's Protection 64

Life after Death 70

The Plan

For I know the thoughts that I think toward you, says the Lord, thoughts of peace and not of evil, to give you a future and a hope.

– Jeremiah 29:11 NKJV

Have you ever wondered, *"Why am I here? What have I been destined to do? How will my life be when I get older? What will I become in life? What is my purpose?"* These are things we often ask ourselves when we already know the answer. We are born with a purpose and a destiny. Sometimes we may not want to accept who or what we are meant to be, but that doesn't stop God's plan. The way has already been made, so we must discover it and walk in it.

Before we were born, God had already instilled in us the gifts and talents that we would need later in life, as affirmed in Jeremiah 1:5 (NKJV). *"Before I formed thee in the belly, I knew thee; and before thou camest forth out of the womb I sanctified thee, and I ordained thee a prophet unto the nations,"* it reads.

God knew who and what we would become; it's up to us to connect to the purpose and let it manifest.

I have always known that I wanted to be an entrepreneur and serve others. Having come from a kindhearted family, it was second nature for me. As I grew up, I watched my grandma feed individuals she didn't know. Even with seven or more grandchildren at the house, and a husband, she invited people from the church or store to come over and eat with us and made sure they were taken care of. I guess I can say I inherited some of her characteristics.

I was reared in the church. My mom made sure we attended Sunday school, Bible class, vacation Bible school, revivals, worship service, and more. All we knew was church. It's funny because when I got older, I wasn't too fond of Sunday school. It was fun and exciting when I was younger, but when I was able to drive myself, it became boring, so I stopped attending. Even with my spiritual upbringing, I strayed from God.

Have you ever wandered from God? How did you feel? Did you feel lost? When I walked away, I felt lost and empty. I was around 23, and I was frustrated with the church. It didn't seem like things were going right in my life, so I wanted to try something different and do my own thing.

Live!

When I made that decision, I knew it was wrong, but I was curious to see what my life would be like if I stopped singing and praying. I wanted to see how it felt to live how I wanted to live and do what I wanted to do, without feeling bad about it. I wanted to be "outside," as the young people would say.

I knew God would not be pleased. I still attended church every Sunday, playing the piano, but outside those doors, I was living my best life, or so I thought. I was living the life of a heathen! I was trapped in my mind, but I thought I had it made. I have never been the type that enjoys going to the club, yet I was fornicating and drinking without repentance, thinking it was okay if I still went to church, but it wasn't.

Holiness was and still is, right in the eyesight of God. My flesh was pleased but my spirit was disconnected and void. The best part about backsliding or falling short is that we still must return to God and get back to the plan He has for us. I was no exception.

Whenever you're disconnected from God, there will be no peace. You may think your life is good, but with God, it's better. I knew I wasn't in right standing with God, and I knew He didn't want me to be in that place.

One thing I promised myself was that I wouldn't stay outside of His will for long. I knew I had to get back in right standing for Him to use me and for me to fulfill my purpose. I was scared because I didn't want God to release His hands from me. I didn't want to stay stuck in sin forever or die in my sin.

I understand that you may want to live a fast life for whatever reason, but it's not worth it. I guarantee you, there's no better way to live life than with Jesus. We should trust in God and be led and directed by whatever He tells us to do.

When we live our life for God and allow Him to lead us, it makes life better. That doesn't mean we won't go through things, but if we do, He will strengthen us in the process to get through it. The Bible tells us that.

Do you know what God requires of you? My daily prayer is that God uses me for His glory and that everything I do pleases Him. It took me 30 years with some heartache, trials, and tribulations, but I can say, I have discovered my purpose. I know what I'm called to do. When you get that revelation, your life will change.

How do you know what you've been destined to do? What is the plan God has for your life? To find out, it takes spending quality time with God. Prepare to commune with Him by fasting and praying. God will tell you exactly what it is He wants you to do.

Everyone has a purpose on earth. One's purpose may be to encourage or assist others. Some may be called to be doctors and lawyers. Some may be called to be veterinarians. Some may be called to preach the Word of God to break the chains of bondage. Whatever it is, God will give you divine instructions on how to accomplish it and operate in that gift.

Blessed are those who hunger and thirst for righteousness, for they shall be filled. – Matthew 5:6 NKJV

Now that you've discovered your purpose, are you willing to go through the process to fulfill it? This is a tough one and please don't be alarmed, but we pray for the glory of God to be revealed in our lives and for us to walk upright with Him, but that doesn't come easily.

Are you prepared for the challenges that come with it? Are you prepared for lying, backbiting, anger, disappointment, and loneliness?

It's all right to answer "no" because no one is ever prepared, but that doesn't stop His plan. God requires more of you! When you decide to live a life pleasing unto the Lord, that is when the enemy's attacks become stronger. Be not alarmed! God will see you through and it's all for His glory.

God wants us to desire more, but it is a process. Don't let the enemy defeat you by telling you to give up or that you can't do it. You are more than a conqueror and you can get through anything that comes against you. If they persecuted Jesus, why would we be exempt? If the anointing was cheap, everyone would have it.

My daily prayer, at one point in life, was that God would let people see Him through me and I would exemplify His characteristics. That's how I wanted to live my life. I thought it was a wonderful and powerful prayer, you know, to be the apple of God's eye.

Until one day trouble knocked on my door and I changed my confession! Yes! I no longer wanted to say that prayer because I allowed my circumstance to hinder what was pleasing to my Father! I no longer wanted what it took for God to be glorified in my life.

When someone or something hurts you to the core, you reconsider a lot. Can I be real for a second? I was hurt and confused. I didn't want to attend church. I didn't have anyone to talk to about what I was going through because no one would believe me. All I could do was return to God and pray. During the process, He reminded me of the prayer I prayed and the confession I made.

He asked, "*Do you not still want to be like Me? If I had to endure, why not you?*" I wanted to be stubborn and remain in my flesh, but I repented, asked for forgiveness, and got back on track. The journey does not come easily when you desire to please God, but do not give up.

Regardless of what we go through in life, we should want to glorify God through it all. I know it gets hard and you get weary along the way, but we can't allow people and situations to make us change our confession. If this happens, repent and return to God.

God is still God and if He brings us to it, He has already prepared the way for us to get through it. Although it hurts going through it, we should know that we will win in the end and have the victory! It pays to be special in God's eyes. I'll forever go through it if, in the end, I win.

Points to Ponder

1 - What is your purpose in life?

_____

_____

_____

2 - Are you comfortable with where you are?

_____

_____

_____

3 - What do you desire from God?

_____

_____

_____

Meditation

Who Am I?

Before I formed you in the womb, I knew you; Before you were born, I sanctified you; I ordained you a prophet to the nations.

– Jeremiah 1:5 NKJV

Are you living your dreams or living the dreams of others? Most of the time we're taking care of others but neglect ourselves. A minister once told me to stay in shape. She said, *"Where God is taking you, you will have to be in shape and in good health."*

Well, it took me years to get the revelation and I have gained a few pounds since we last talked. Now that I'm reminded of what God said, I must get in position. Some may not believe in prophecies or spoken words from God, but I do.

Live!

When God speaks, you should obey. There is no question about it. When God has ordained you for something, He wants to make sure you're able to carry out the task. He will not tell us to do something that we cannot do. We must get guidance and instructions from Him. What have you done with what He has given you?

Oftentimes, people get labeled at an early age. Some may hear they will never be anything. Some may hear, "You will be just like your dad! No good!" Do not let that stop you from being whom God has called you to be. If God was able to deliver those people in the Bible, He can do it for us.

For someone who has come from an abusive home, whether verbally or physically, you have a purpose. For someone who grew up in a single-parent home, you have a purpose. To that little boy or girl who was molested but couldn't tell anyone, you have a purpose. To that former prostitute or drug addict, you have a purpose! *Everyone* has a purpose!

Take it from me—Arletha, whom everyone calls Vonda. I was reared in Flora, a small town in Mississippi. I am the eldest of three.

Growing up, I knew God had a purpose for my life, but I wasn't sure what it was. I started playing the piano for a church when I was 15 years old and was a full-time musician a year later.

If you're a musician, or familiar with the lifestyle, then you understand that's a big task at such a young age. My dad always said, "As long as you know how to play the piano, you'll never go broke!"

In 2000, at the age of 16, I was making a minimum of $600 a month. I thought I was rich! Being able to make my own money at a young age, without the stress of a job, instilled entrepreneurship in me. I knew then that one day I would want to be a boss and have a company that would become worldwide.

But before I was making the "big bucks," I had dreams of becoming a teacher in middle school. My grandad would always get me to read his mail to him or give me a spelling contest, although he could never spell the words. He would always call me his schoolteacher. I would read it twice, sometimes three times, to make sure he understood.

By the time I got to high school, I changed my mind and wanted to be a pediatrician. Needless to say, neither worked.

My aunt bought a computer, and I would visit her just to play on it and print things. If she ever had problems with the computer, she would call me to fix it. From there, I started a business/hobby and I called it Vonda's Graphics.

I didn't know much about entrepreneurship at the time, but I was determined to be different. All I knew was that I was destined to do great things.

Live!

I started out making business cards and programs for local churches and business owners. No one in my family was an entrepreneur because we were always taught to go to school, get a good education, and get a good job. I, on the other hand, knew there was more.

I went to school to be a Certified Nurse Assistant and Registered Nurse but didn't pursue the career. Finally, I decided to do Health Information Technology (HIT). With HIT, I was able to work in the medical field as well as on the computer. I was excited. I knew I had found my career because computers and electronics were my things.

Fast forward to 23, I gave birth to my beautiful daughter. I didn't know anything about being a mother. I was afraid and nervous. This was not the plan I had for my life, but that's what it was. You see, I was the quiet church girl, and getting pregnant without being married was not part of the plan. I was upset with myself, but I knew I wanted to love her and create the perfect world for her.

While pregnant, the doctor told me my baby would be born with sickle cell anemia. I didn't want that for her. Every morning, I would lay hands on my stomach and pray for her. I asked God to give me the wisdom to care for her and to let her have a healthy, good life.

After I gave birth, she was blessed. She never had to stay in the hospital overnight or never had blood transfusions, which is all normal in sickle cell patients.

Arletha Orr

God favored her! She was healthy, happy, and spoiled!

Before I met my husband, I had given up on being married. I was just 27 years old, but I thought I was too old and figured no one would want a woman with a baby who was not theirs. I told God I was done trying it my way and would trust Him.

Then, He decided to bless us with a husband and dad. In May 2012, I met the man of my dreams and we married in May 2013. While dating, we never argued.

Neither one of us liked confusion. He never had a problem doing anything for me or my baby. Although he had two daughters, he treated my baby as his own. Whatever we needed, he was always there.

God had sent the perfect man! He spent time with our daughter, taught her how to ride her bike, assisted with homework, and raked leaves. One time she made a daring statement, saying, "Mama, Daddy's cooking tastes better than yours!" I laughed but gladly accepted it. So, as you can see, he did most of the cooking as well.

In 2014, God said my family was not complete and He decided to add to #TeamAllen. On December 31, 2014, we birthed an active, bouncy baby boy. *Oh, boy! Oh, boy!* We all wanted a male child and were so glad when he arrived. Some people say little boys are "bad," but I wouldn't say that. I just think they're more active and

Live!

curious. Man! Our son was very loving, caring, and energetic.

After our wedding, I decided to do event planning, a skill my "play mom" instilled in me at 21. My husband was there every step of the way. Oh, how I miss those days. I wouldn't do any of the liftings. All I would do was set up and he handled the rest.

I had the perfect family, the perfect plan, and the perfect story. I did not see all this coming for my life. I was happy. They were happy. Although that's only the beginning, I knew it was more to come. I am a mother, a wife, and an entrepreneur. Who are *you*?

If you have special dreams and desires, discover your purpose and go for it! Don't let anyone or any situation stop you from going forth. Deep inside, you know what you're destined to do but you're afraid. I want to remind you that you've never lost it. Face your fear! Get up and go after what God has called you to do! He will lead you on the right path.

I remember when I was young, I used to have dreams and visions, but I had no idea what they meant. I would think, *Why am I having these dreams that become reality? Who is this being He has made me?* It was when I got older and began to study the Bible, that I knew what my destiny would be.

Arletha Orr

God knows EVERYTHING about you! Even after you learn what you're supposed to do, He still has more to teach and show you. Trust Him in the process.

Points to Ponder

1 - Who are YOU?

_____

_____

_____

2 - Who or what do you aspire to be?

_____

_____

_____

3 - Are you doing what God has called you to do?

_____

_____

_____

Meditation

Sanctification & The Anointing

And you shall take the anointing oil, pour it on his head, and anoint him.

– *Exodus 29:7 NKJV*

Growing up, we were taught that you could pretty much sin and do what you wanted, if you went to church. What is sin? Sin is any act or words we say that wouldn't be pleasing in the eyesight of God. We were taught salvation, but not sanctification. When we saw a certain group of people dressed a certain way or acting a certain way, we classified them as being "sanctified!"

Sanctified people wore dresses all the time and they could not wear makeup. They stayed in the church for at least four hours each time they went. Our perception of being sanctified was wrong. What is being sanctified or sanctification? According to Webster, sanctification means "the state of being sanctified, which means to be free from sin, purified, holiness."

Wow! Our way of life and what we were taught was the opposite of that. Now, I'm not throwing stones at anyone, because I truly believe we were taught what the elders knew and understood, but I knew it had to be something greater.

"Church folks" pay our tithes faithfully every Sunday yet we're struggling, trying to make ends meet. You do what is required but it seems like it's never enough. You want to give up on life because nothing seems to go right but something on the inside keeps telling you to keep moving forward. There must be a better way and it is, so don't give up! You're almost there.

God wants us to live in abundance. Ephesians 3:20 (NKJV) states, *"Now to Him who is able to do exceedingly abundantly above all that we ask or think, according to the power that works in us."*

With salvation and sanctification comes the Holy Spirit, which is why you desire to be righteous and set aside, and why you long for more. It is His job to comfort and encourage you.

When you get discouraged, isn't it amazing how the Holy Spirit comes in and uplifts us? God reminds us of His

Live!

Word and His promise, and then we're strengthened to move forward in Him.

As John 14:26 (NKJV), reminds us, "*But the Helper, the Holy Spirit, whom the Father will send in My name, He will teach you all things, and bring to your remembrance all things that I said to you.*"

If you're not saved, you can get saved today. Accept Jesus into your life. Romans 10:9 (NKJV) encourages us, "*That if you confess with your mouth the Lord Jesus and believe in your heart that God has raised Him from the dead, you will be saved.*"

What does that mean exactly? If you confess that Jesus is Lord, believe in your heart in the death, burial, and resurrection of Jesus, you shall be saved. All your sins have been forgiven. It's not hard and it's free! Accept Him as your Lord today.

So now we've grown from the churchgoer to walking in righteousness, and we are ready for the things of God. I wasn't sure if I was saved, so I decided to get rebaptized. I wanted to be sure.

Baptism is when you've been immersed in water, and it symbolizes the washing away of your sins or purification. The Holy Spirit doesn't dwell in an unclean temple.

Keep in mind that, although you're in right standing with God, it doesn't mean you won't go through trials and tribulations. When we face those giants, they're only to make us stronger.

Our faith must be tested for us to elevate in our walk with Christ. God wants us to live in abundance; therefore, growth is required. The question is, what will be required for your growth?

The anointing is the outpouring of God's spirit on His chosen vessels. During Biblical times, when someone was anointed to do something, they were specifically chosen by God or God's leaders. When you're anointed, you have been specifically handpicked by God to perform a task.

Sometimes we are afraid of that word, as we should be because the anointing is not to be taken lightly. It is God's stamp of approval for you to do what He has ordained you to do. This takes us back to our purpose and how God has anointed us to fulfill it.

What has God anointed you to do? Most of the time when we think about these questions, our mind goes to preaching. Your calling or purpose does not have to be inside of the church. You can be anointed to do jail or street ministry. God can use you to do numerous things.

He has placed inside of us what we need. It's up to us to activate it and put it to work. We must fast and pray to receive revelation on what God wants us to do and to fulfill it.

Live!

Please understand, this journey won't be easy. It comes with challenges and obstacles but in the end, God is glorified and you're drawing people to the Kingdom of God.

Points to Ponder

1 - Are you saved?

_____

_____

_____

2 - What has God anointed you to do?

_____

_____

_____

3 - Are you ready to walk in your calling?

_____

_____

_____

Meditation

Prayer

Father, I pray that whoever reads this chapter will accept you as their Lord and Savior, and let You reign and rule in their life if they haven't already. For without You, we can't do anything. It is through the Holy Spirit that we are strengthened and healed.

Forgive them of their sins. Reside in their hearts and minds so that they may do things pleasing in Your sight and live a righteous life. Anoint us, God, so that we're able to do what You have called us to do.

Cleanse and purify our hearts and minds, so that we can have a clean slate to praise and worship you. God, purify our mouth and ear gates so that we can speak those things which are holy and only hear what is pure.

God, we cancel every distraction that the enemy brings our way. We will stay focused on You. Our lives will line up with Your Word that we may draw others unto the Kingdom of God. Have Your way in our lives and let Your will be done forever. In Jesus's name, amen.

The Heartbreak

Be strong. Take courage. Don't be intimidated. Don't give them a second thought because GOD, your God, is striding ahead of you. He's right there with you. He won't let you down; he won't leave you.

— Deuteronomy 31:6 MSG

When you pray and ask God for more of Him and the things of God, be prepared for the territory that comes with it. God gave His only Son so that the world could be saved. What are you willing to go through or experience so that you can help draw people to the Kingdom of God?

Never in a million years did I think I would have to endure a tragedy. Why? Because I'm the lady that goes to church every Sunday, sings in the choir, preaches the Word of

God, and plays the piano. God said, "PERFECT! You are the person I can use."

I was at a point in my life where I desired more of God because I knew I had a purpose, and that was my daily prayer. Everything goes well in our life until tragedy hits. What if everything you worked hard to build slipped through your fingers and disappeared? You may be thinking, *How did I miss it?* When things often happen in our life, our favorite questions are, "What did I do to cause it?" or "Why me?" The answer is, not a thing. God is sovereign and His perfect will has to be done.

Remember my perfect and happy family? I lost it all. I can't tell you anything about being abused, molested, or being a drug user, but I can tell you how I survived my heart being ripped from my chest with no air to breathe.

As stated earlier, my prayer was that God would use me for His glory. I wanted people to see God through me, and I still do. Was I prepared for the process that needed to take place for me to grow? Ahh, absolutely not!

The anointing comes with a cost. Please don't misunderstand. We're not sacrificing anything for greater power, but when God gets ready to elevate you, He must make sure you can handle it.

Why give me eight million dollars, when I can't manage $800? Do not be alarmed because God desires us to want more. He doesn't want us dead spiritually and not

Live!

growing. Everything that has life, grows! I remind myself that if it happens, I know God has me covered and will see me through it.

I remember so well; it was a sunny Wednesday morning, the alarm went off at 6:00, and I jumped to my feet. I called my children's names and then said, "Wake up! It's time to go to school."

My baby girl would run into my bedroom and hug the life out of me. It was such an amazing feeling. My son would wake up, rub his eyes, and say, "Ma, eat eat!"

This was the beginning of my awesome day! This morning was no different from any other. We got up, got breakfast, got dressed, had our conversations, playtime, and were on our way to start our day.

Never take life for granted because all that could change in the twinkling of an eye. I've never been a person of conflict and I would encourage you to adopt similar characteristics. Don't argue with people. If you are in conflict with someone, resolve the issue and don't hold grudges.

I know we all get upset and have disagreements, but once you disagree, makeup and get back in good standing with each other. You never know when it may be your last time with them. Love on everyone!

Arletha Orr

Who would've known that would be the last morning I would spend with my children? The last time I would ever dress or feed them. The last time I would embrace their warm hugs and kisses. The last time I would drop them off at school and tell them I love them. The last time I would hear, "Mommy, I love you!"

You see, we had a loving and caring family. My husband would pick up the kids mostly from the daycare center. He worked overnight, and I worked the normal eight to five, so we made it work. Every school function or church event, we were in attendance as a family.

Of course, we had our disagreements from time to time, but we never went to bed upset with each other. We apologized and made sure the issue was resolved before we laid our heads down to rest.

In 2016, my life changed forever. I was about to get off work but needed to stay a little longer. My husband called, and he said he would pick up the babies from daycare. I said, "Cool, I'll stay a little longer at work to finish up."

I left around 5:30. It seemed to be a normal day, as stated earlier, but then my phone rang. I answered, and a woman told me, "Your husband has been hit by a train!"

You'd be amazed at how much your brain can process in such a little time. I was shocked. Nervous. In disbelief. Heartbroken. Sad. I thought to myself, *But he has the kids. This can't be true. Could she have identified the wrong vehicle? Could*

Live!

she have thought it was someone else? Could she have the wrong phone number?

My heart started palpitating, as I began to sweat and gasp for air. By this time, I was five minutes from my house. I didn't know what to do. The caller described his vehicle and told me where to come. I immediately turned around and went to the location. I couldn't believe what I heard.

As I drove, I prayed. I didn't want it to be true. I didn't want it to be my family or anyone else's. *Maybe it was someone else with a similar vehicle*, I thought. *Oh, God! But someone was hit! Someone was hurt!*

I arrived and got out of my truck, and then walked towards the scene of the accident. My heart was literally about to jump out of my chest, as I saw my husband's red truck on the track—almost in pieces.

When I saw familiar faces, I knew it had to be them. If you're a parent, you understand that our first instinct when we see our child hurt, is to rescue them. All I wanted to do was run to the train track and get my babies out of the truck, but I was too late.

My husband had picked our children up from daycare and as they were en route to our home, they were struck by an Amtrak train. My heart immediately dropped! You can imagine the thoughts that were going through my mind. *What? God this is not happening! This can't be real!*

Although I wouldn't wish this upon my worst enemy, if I had one, I was praying it was all a dream. This couldn't possibly be happening to us. I had just spoken with my husband less than an hour ago.

Standing, with tears flowing down my face, I watched and waited on them to get them out, hoping and praying that someone would resuscitate them and save them. They told me the ambulance was on their way to take them to the hospital. They told me they would be okay. They told me, they told me—but it never happened.

Maybe one person will be okay if not all. This will all be over soon, I assured myself. *We may have to spend some nights in the hospital, but we will make it.* Death NEVER crossed my mind.

There was no ambulance in sight. No one came. I had arrived about 10 to 15 minutes after they were struck, and the ambulance arrived maybe ten minutes after I got there. No one came to their rescue. I wondered, *Would it have been better if they arrived earlier?*

I stood, as a mother and a wife, hoping that I would have the opportunity to nurse and love on my family later. I did the only thing I knew to do and that was praying. When you don't know what to do, you do what you know to do. I prayed in the Holy Spirit because I didn't know what to say. That's all that would come out of my mouth.

Live!

"Likewise, the Spirit also helps in our weaknesses. For we do not know what we should pray for as we ought, but the Spirit Himself makes intercession for us with groanings which cannot be uttered," Romans 8:26 (NKJV) tells us.

There I was, praying in the Holy Spirit, and standing with tears in my eyes, flowing down my face. I was still hoping and praying that the first responders would get my family to the hospital so that I could see them. I prayed that I could hug and kiss them and tell them everything would be okay.

Hurry, people, hurry! I thought, *My family needs you! Where is the medical backup? Who's coming to save them?* I stared at the truck on the tracks and waited.

And waited.

And waited.

The ambulance finally arrived and pulled my husband out and laid him on the ground. I thought, *This can't be good, but since they got him out, now they can go to the hospital and receive care. They'll be okay.* But they weren't

Arletha Orr

A few moments later, the Chief of Police stood before me and said, "I'm sorry, ma'am, but your husband and child are gone!"

I thought, *Where is my baby!?* Another officer pulled him to the side and corrected him. He said there were two children. The chief then corrected himself. I thought for a second that they had lost my baby boy or that he was ejected from the truck, and they could not find him.

To this day, I don't have clarity because I never went back to ask. I can only imagine having to tell someone that news, but at that moment, I felt like my heart was snatched from my chest. I felt the life leave my body. I couldn't believe it! I didn't believe him! I wanted to go get my babies, but they wouldn't let me. I was heartless. I was broken. I was confused. I was empty. I was dead.

I was perplexed. I had no words. I couldn't talk. He stood, asking questions, but I could not answer. My aunt was there, and she answered the questions for me. I felt as if I had died. My babies were gone. My husband was gone. Everything I had was gone. No, I wasn't prepared for it and didn't think this would happen to me, but it did.

It finally resonated that I couldn't save them. I couldn't identify them. They wouldn't let me see them, but I knew I wasn't leaving until I knew my babies were off that track and safe.

Live!

I stood, as people gathered—the community, the news station, my family—everybody. The funeral home came, and that eased me a little bit. I wept for hours and hours and hours. All I could think was that my family was gone. They were my everything and all I had! I was so grateful to have a loving family, friends, and a community to pray for me when I couldn't pray for myself.

That night, before bed, I prayed and asked God to cover me and allow me to rest. I think it was so traumatic to where I was in another world. *Was I on earth?* I don't know. I knew I didn't have my babies and it hurt. My mom wouldn't let me go home so I stayed at her house, but God allowed me to rest.

Points to Ponder

1 - What are some things that you hold dear to your heart that you don't want to lose?

_____

_____

_____

2 - What have you lost that's hard to accept?

_____

_____

_____

3 - If something traumatic or tragic happened today, could you be at peace?

_____

_____

_____

Meditation

Broken but Healed

I shall not die, but live, and declare the works of the Lord.

— Psalms 118:17 KJV

I still thought that my situation wasn't real and that it couldn't be happening.

Am I dreaming? God made a mistake, right?! Maybe the police should go back and check again? This can't be real. This isn't my life! That's not my family! Someone wake me up from this horrible dream. Then I thought, *Could I have prepared for this? What could I have done differently that morning?*

I began to reflect on my life and my "good deeds." I attend church every Sunday. I give my tithes and offerings. I'm loyal to my husband and I'm the best mom this world could offer, so why me, God? This cannot happen to me!

Live!

When I tell you, I've never felt pain like that before in my life; it was unbearable and unthinkable.

I felt bitter, broken, hurt, and betrayed.

Why had God allowed this to happen to me? It felt as if someone had reached into my thoracic cavity and snatched my heart out. My family was my everything and now, in a split second, they were no longer here.

Growing up, the older people used to tell us not to question God, and I'm pretty sure you've heard the same. When you're going through things in life and you can't find the answers anywhere, you have no choice but to question or talk to Him about it. Who else can you talk to? I think God is okay—well, I *know* God is okay with us questioning Him to get a better understanding of why things happen in our life. He desires to have a relationship with us.

The day after the accident, I was lying on the couch at my mom's house. I was crying so hard that my chest was hurting, and I could not breathe. I cried and cried so much, I was gasping for air. During times like these, the family can't comfort you because they're in disbelief and wailing themselves, so you have no one to turn to but God.

Don't get me wrong; my family was there every step of the way, but there are some voids man cannot fill. I asked

Arletha Orr

God, "What do I do? How will I live my life without my family?"

Everything that I lived for had been snatched away from me! I had nothing. My everyday routine was to drop the children off at school, go to work and come home, and be a wife and mother. *God, where do I go from here? How do I go on with my life?*

I laid there in silence and God spoke to me in a quiet, still voice and said, "They're okay, and you will be okay."

So, I said, "God, what will I do without them?"

That quiet, still voice said, "LIVE!"

What? Live? How? That's not possible. I'm already living.

He said it again, "LIVE!"

I rose from the couch, dried my eyes, smiled, and went outside. When you're going through, everybody says they understand, and that "everything will be okay," but when you hear it from God, that's when it has substance! That's when you know it's real and no one can take that from you.

After He spoke, I was at peace. That may sound strange to some, but I knew God was with me and covering me. Although I was heartbroken, I acknowledged that God is sovereign, and He doesn't make mistakes.

Live!

It was time to prepare for their homegoing celebration. Visiting the funeral home was unreal. From the date of the accident, I had probably gone three to four or maybe even five times with my mom, and it wasn't easy.

Visiting the funeral home before the week of the funeral, I was okay. Knowing that they were close but not actually in the ground gave me some sense of relief because I knew I could see them again.

Before we went each time, I always prayed and asked God to give me strength. It was only through the power of the Holy Spirit that I made it through. My family assisted in preparing the attire and programs. I could not have done it alone.

The morning of the funeral was challenging. I didn't want to go. I felt empty. This would be my last time seeing them. There would be no more funeral home visits; this was it.

I was crushed and didn't think I would make it through the day. I remember eating breakfast, praying, and dragging my feet to get dressed. I knew it had to be done but I didn't want to do it.

I didn't want a traditional funeral. I wanted it to be a celebration! I wanted us to sing, dance, and shout because all of them were full of life and enjoyed their life to the fullest. And *yes*, we celebrated!

Arletha Orr

It was the best homegoing celebration I ever attended. It wasn't sad at all. We went in and gave God praise!

I knew in my heart my family would have wanted that; how dare I not give it to them? No one could see it, but I put my daughter's favorite boots on her, and put my son's favorite toy in the casket as well. I wanted them to leave with the items they loved the most.

Although I faced confusion with some people, I did what I knew my family would have wanted me to do. You wouldn't think that people would be so evil or coldhearted during times of tragedy, but they were. I was stunned by some of their behavior, but I thank God for that as well.

My husband and my children were always positive and loving individuals. They always saw the best in people, even when they had wicked ways. It would have been a disservice to them had I not done the right thing for their celebration.

Hearing from God assures us that everything will be good, and no one can take that from us. When you hear from God, that doesn't mean everything will be great, but I guarantee, you will be fine.

Although I received that Word from God, something still felt like it wasn't adding up. I thought because God had spoken, I wouldn't have to face the heartache, disappointment, agony, denial, and shock. I guess for a minute, I thought I was invincible.

Live!

I was incorrect. You see, we are still human beings and that comes with feelings and emotions. I still had to face those feelings and the first one was denial.

Denial means that you refuse to believe something, and you feel isolated because of what has happened. I know that God doesn't make mistakes, but I felt betrayed and isolated. I could not believe it. I was still in total shock. I felt alone.

I was an ordinary lady who loved her family. I was the typical good girl. So, I couldn't understand why it had to happen to me. I began to blame myself. I wondered if I had done anything to cause it.

My body was numb. I heard and saw visitors come in and out but didn't hear or see anyone. My emotions and feelings were dead. Friends and family came to the house, but I vaguely remember them. I was there and interacted with them, but mentally, I was a zombie. I was lost. I was alone. I was heartbroken. All I could hear was that voice saying, "LIVE!"

Although I had my mom and friends around, I didn't have my crew, the #TeamAllen crew. I was missing parts of me that no one else could feel. I was missing parts that I never knew could leave me.

As the days and weeks passed, I got discouraged. Every time I felt as if I was sinking, I would hear, "LIVE!" Isn't it amazing how we start feeling like there's no hope for us, but God speaks a Word? He's AH-MAZING!

The more I heard it, the more strength I gained, the better I felt, and the more I felt life in my body!

Although I knew I would be sad, I didn't want to get to the point where I would slip into depression. Every time I became sad, I would pray and ask God to give me the strength to keep moving. I'm a minister and psalmist, so you would think I would pick up the Bible and read it to feed my spirit, you know, to give me hope.

It didn't happen. I was at a point where I could not do it. I couldn't even pray. I'm glad others were praying for me. All I could do was eat, sleep, sing, and in the midst of it all, I continued to call on Jesus. If I didn't know how to do anything else, I could do that, and it didn't take a year for Him to restore me.

I knew God was with me, but I couldn't explain that to others. I remember people would come to me and begin to cry and I would be smiling because I knew God had me covered! I felt as if God had me in a bubble. I called it grieving in the Holy Ghost! Smile! All I knew to do was to pray and give Him praise.

I didn't want to cry day after day because I knew if I would have allowed myself to go there, I could've easily slipped into a slump, and I didn't want that for my life. I knew my family wouldn't want it for me either. I remember telling

Live!

God, "That same Holy Ghost that I preach and sing about, I need it to activate immediately in my life and give me strength!"

I needed Him to show Himself mighty. Yes, I would cry some nights, but I would play *You are My Strength* by William Murphy and Jesus would rock me to sleep. Oh, what a blessing it is to be wrapped in the arms of Jesus and allow Him to console you when you're going through.

Points to Ponder

1 - What has God spoken to you?

_____

_____

_____

2 - What are you in denial about?

_____

_____

_____

3 - Are you ready to be healed?

_____

_____

_____

Meditation

Resentment & Shock

Let all bitterness, wrath, anger, clamor, and evil speaking, be put away from you, with all malice.

— *Ephesians 4:31 NKJV*

As time progressed, I started attending church again. I may have only missed one or two Sundays. Although I was going through, He was still deserving of my praise and worship. That's how you know God is with you when you're going through it, and you still have a heart and mind to give Him your best.

Church was good for a couple of weeks. It was the norm. Then, it changed. Everywhere I went, whether church or on the radio, there would be someone that says, "Give Him praise because He's about to turn things around for your family!"

Live!

I would have this nonchalant attitude and say, "For what? I don't have a family! I'm not praising God for a family when I don't have one and I'm not praising Him for someone else's. You know what? I'll stay quiet and not open my mouth because God took my family. I don't have to say a word." Wow!

I didn't realize it at the time, but the enemy crept in and started to build resentment in my heart towards God. The same God whom I stated was sovereign and deserving of praise. The same God whom had spoken and told me to live. The same God who I recognized as being God. The same God who sent the Holy Ghost to comfort me in my time of need. Every time I heard something about family, I would frown. I didn't want to hear anything about a family.

Not only was I being rebellious in my worship, but I was still shocked. Here it was, three months later, and I was still in shock. Yes, it was a very traumatic accident, and I couldn't believe that God allowed that to happen to me. Me? I'm the good church girl but God had other plans.

Let me be the first to tell you that was very selfish of me. That was not right and not pleasing in God's sight. When God revealed to me how I was thinking and reacting, I immediately repented to God for my foolish ways and asked for forgiveness. Don't ignore God when He shows you, you. It's all part of the purification process.

How dare I act like that towards the One that gave me life? How dare I act like that towards the One who gives me breath to still wake up every morning? How dare I act like that towards the One that has allowed me to still be in my right mind? Y'all, I was upset with myself, to know that I even thought like that.

What if it was *me* in the train accident? God spared my life, and I was being selfish. He left me here, so I know my purpose hadn't been fulfilled. Please don't misunderstand me. I love my family and I'm not saying they didn't have a purpose, but God has His perfect will, and it must go as He plans.

Devastated and heartbroken, I knew that I had to live for them and myself, so I began to wonder and think, what is *my* purpose?

The enemy has tried to place other thoughts in my mind as well, to go against God. When I recognize it, I cast it down. I pray and ask God to remove those thoughts that are not of Him. God had to perform spiritual surgery on me to renew my heart and my mind. My thoughts were not of God. I was broken but healed! I resented God, but He still restored my mind!

LIVE! LIVE! LIVE!

Points to Ponder

1 - What grudges are you holding in your heart for what God has done?

_____

_____

_____

2 - Are you willing to be led by the Holy Spirit?

_____

_____

_____

3 - Do you feel you can forgive and move forward?

_____

_____

_____

Meditation

Come out of Lo-debar

He will redeem his soul from going down to the pit, and his life shall see the light.

– Job 33:28 NKJV

It got hard during the holidays, especially Christmas of 2016. At the beginning of the week, I didn't want to be bothered. I didn't want to leave my house. I wanted to stay in the bed and hide under my covers the entire day.

Christmas is a family holiday, and my babies would wake up, open their gifts, and play. To see the smiles on their faces when you've made their day is priceless. Parents, you know the feeling, but I no longer had that to look forward to.

I decided that I wasn't going to call or visit anyone. I wanted to be alone. Ha! I was planning all of this in my mind. I told myself that I would have a miserable day.

How crazy is that? But isn't it amazing how God steps in right when you need Him to? I wanted to do one thing, but His plan was something else. I would say about midweek, I started feeling refreshed and alive and my mindset changed!

No longer did I want to be alone, but I wanted to spend Christmas with my family, the people that I loved. Although I didn't have my immediate family, I had other families to love. How dare I not cherish those moments with them? I survived through Christmas with a smile!

When birthdays and other holidays came, I decided to take a different approach. Instead of making myself sad and isolating myself from others, I decided to do something to make myself happy. I decided to reroute my thoughts. I didn't want to be depressed, replaying that day through my mind, thinking about the funeral, or thinking about them and making myself cry. I wanted to *live*! I wanted to break that cycle over my life, and I want to break it over yours as well.

I encourage and challenge you to reroute your feelings. I see a lot of people post on social media about the anniversary of someone's death. Why do that? Don't replay the day they left or the day of the funeral, by pulling

Live!

pictures from 10 years ago. I knew my family would want me to be happy and loving life, and I'm sure your loved one would want the same. Do something for yourself! Love on yourself! I promise you will feel better.

I know it's hard around those times, but no longer will you be sad or depressed. You will live an abundant life and do what God has called you to do. You are still here for a purpose! Walk-in what God has called you to do! It's okay to get sad, but don't stay in Lo-debar forever.

In the Bible, Lo-debar means a place of nothing—no pasture, no word, and no communication. Why should you dwell in a place of nothingness, when you have life and have it more abundantly? Come out of Lo-debar and come to the land of good!

Tell those dry bones and dead thoughts to LIVE! You have the power to speak that over yourself. It wasn't your fault that you lost someone dear to your heart. God is sovereign and has a plan. Thank God for the time He blessed you with that loved one. All of us have to return to Him one day. Life is not eternal. Today, you will live and not die and declare the works of the Lord!

Points to Ponder

1 - Who or what is keeping you in bondage?

_____

_____

_____

2 - Are you ready to live an abundant life?

_____

_____

_____

3 - How will you let go and let God have His way in your life?

_____

_____

_____

Meditation

God's Protection

No weapon formed against you shall prosper, and every tongue which rises against you in judgment you shall condemn. This is the heritage of the servants of the Lord, and their righteousness is from Me, says the Lord.

— Isaiah 54:17 NKJV

I've always had dreams and visions, but at first, I didn't quite understand them. I couldn't understand for the life of me how I would see things and then they disappear, or I would dream something, and it would happen. This is not something that was taught to me in my upbringing, so I was clueless as to what it was or what to do about it.

My baby was diagnosed with sickle cell anemia, inutero. This terrified me as a first-time single mom. I did the

Live!

necessary tests to make sure the doctor was correct, and everything led me in the direction that she would have it. Although I still had hope that she wouldn't, she did.

As a new parent, I didn't know how to accept that. All I knew was that I didn't want a sick baby. While pregnant, every day on my way to school, I would lay my hands on my stomach and pray. I would pray for her healing and God's protection over us, to help me be the mom that I would need to be to provide for her.

I began to research this illness to learn more. Someone with sickle cell anemia is said to have episodes of pain, swelling of the hands and feet, strokes, hospitalization for long periods, and blood transfusions. This was horrifying news. I wanted the best for my child, and I wanted her to have and live a healthy life.

I continued to pray, and God told me she would be fine. Out of her seven years of life, my baby was never hospitalized for a sickle cell crisis, never had a blood transfusion, stroke, or anything. God had us covered!

Before she turned one, I had a dream that she wouldn't live past that age. I can't remember the dream in detail, but I remembered the results. She was diagnosed with sickle cell anemia, so I thought that would be the reason.

After that dream, I began to pray and ask God to let me keep her. I didn't want to lose my baby. Then I realized I was being selfish. I told God that if He had to take her, I would be okay with that because I knew He would give me the strength I needed to make it through.

My daughter's first birthday came, and she was still with me. I was on pins and needles. I was so nervous, no joke because my previous dreams and visions had come true. Birthday after birthday, seven years later, she was still with me.

Elders used to say, *"If you dream of a girl, it will be a boy. If you dream of a man, it will be a woman."*

I don't know how true that is or can be, but didn't they have a way of putting things? She was with me all those years and I was truly grateful that He didn't take her.

About three days after the accident, God reminded me of the dream.

I laughed and said, "Okay, Lord!" The dream I had was my firstborn being taken away at age one, but at the time of the accident, my second born was one year old. So, God had prepared me for the day I lost them, seven years ago!

Isn't it amazing how God won't allow things to slip up on you? I'm still amazed at that. When you have the Holy Ghost, nothing is a mystery to you. To some, that may seem strange, and it may be a bit much, but I want you to know that God has your best interest at heart, and He makes us aware of things.

Live!

Had God not prepared me then and reminded me, I don't know how I would have reacted when the accident occurred.

I don't know how much I can stress the goodness and faithfulness of my God. He's awesome! God gave me a warning eight years ago for what would happen eight years later. Amazing! He's not a man that He should lie, so He had to keep His word. I'm grateful that I did not have to be admitted anywhere or take any medication. He takes care of His own.

God will let you know about some things that will happen in your life. In 2008, He was preparing my mind for what would happen in 2016. Yes, it still hurt, but because I knew what He had already shown me, I immediately knew He was protecting me. That gave me some extra hope, faith, and courage to keep going.

I'm not sure of your belief, but God is awesome! He will prepare you for things when you're least expecting them. Don't ignore what God shows you. Whether it is good or bad, pray and ask for His guidance on what to do and how to handle it. He is all-knowing and remarkable and He's ready to protect you through any storm you may go through.

Points to Ponder

1 - Has God shown you anything and it came true?

_____

_____

_____

2 - Do you feel God has been protecting you?

_____

_____

_____

3 - When God gives you a vision or dream, what do you do with it?

_____

_____

_____

Meditation

Life after Death

By no means do I count myself an expert in all of this, but I've got my eye on the goal, where God is beckoning us onward – to Jesus. I'm off and running, and I'm not turning back.

– Philippians 3:14 MSG

We get through these tragic events and face the funeral, but there is still life after death. When all the calls end and the people stop visiting, what do we do? When everything is over, and you are faced with reality—the fact you won't see your loved one again—that's when it hits hard. We must search deep within ourselves to find that place with God to help us to start functioning as we should.

Live!

You may be feeling the same as I have felt. When you want to feel alone, and God is trying to make it better, don't have a pity party. Shake yourself loose.

Lose yourself of the bondage. Lose yourself of the pain. Lose yourself of the heartache. Lose yourself of the agony and stress. Lose yourself of the betrayal and LIVE! That's what our Father requires of us.

We are all here on borrowed time. When someone leaves us, it's all in God's plan and timing. That's why I have chosen to live every day like it's my last day. One thing I am excited about is that my family was saved. They all held a special place in Jesus' heart. It's an awesome feeling to know I steered them in the right direction in their time here on earth. I loved them and spent time with them, so I have no regrets. I know my loves are resting and one day we will meet again.

For the family you have left, how will you impact their lives? Salvation is free to anyone who will receive it. Love is free. Being kind is free. Smiling is free. When God calls you home, will you be ready? Are you saved? Is your family saved? Let's focus on our purpose of why God left us here.

A couple of months after the accident, I got really sad one day. I was crying and screaming at the top of my lungs. This is when I was crying out to God, asking Him, why? I was driving, and I almost had an accident. So then, the enemy began to play with my mind. I begin to wonder, *Why not die? My family is gone. I have nothing to live for.*

I thought if I would die that day, I would be able to be with my family and we could be together again. Immediately, I heard my baby say, "Mama, it's not your time! You have a purpose!" All I could do was cry.

So why did God take my family and leave me here? Why did God take your mom, dad, sister, or brother, and leave you here? What have you been ordained to do? I know I've asked that a couple of times, but I need you to think about it. I know God is sovereign and He has the power to do what He wants, but I'm also aware that His plan must be fulfilled.

Don't be angry with God when things happen in your life. He's God and He knows what's best for you. We are so special to Him that even when we mess up, His promises are still the same towards us. Remember: He created you, and He already knows what will happen in your life before it happens.

After the accident, I begin to seek the face of God, asking Him, "What am I to do?" It's amazing how God will use things to get our attention. Little signs, numbers, or anything else to confirm what He has already spoken.

When God is speaking to you and leading you to do something, you must trust Him and take Him at His Word. Numbers 23:19 (NKJV) states, *"God is not a man,*

Live!

that He should lie, nor a son of man, that He should repent. Has He said, and will He not do? Or has He spoken, and will He not make it good?"

Sometimes people would talk to me and repeat the same thing God said. Be careful, because some people will tell you what they want you to know, and not God. You can rest assured, knowing it's Him by it agreeing with His Word and with what He has already told you.

When it's God, you have no other choice but to accept what He is saying and begin to walk in it. He will make sure He gets the Word to you. Sometimes we want to ignore Him, but He will always send a reminder.

To move or go forward after the process, there will be some testing of your faith. I'm reminded of when the serpent tempted Eve in the Bible. Although God gave the command to Adam, the enemy still came to snatch what God said.

It may seem as if the ones you trusted the most will betray you, but stay the course. God is still working. Here's how I see it, when we're being tested or going through trials, especially when you know you're on the right path, the enemy is out to steal what God has put in you.

Sometimes you may give in and step off of course for a little while, but make sure you get back on the right track. We all make mistakes. I cannot tell you I have always done it right. The enemy will send distractions.

The Bible says, in Proverbs 24:16 (NKJV), *for a righteous man may fall seven times and rise again, but the wicked shall fall by calamity.* When I got unfocused and wanted to do things on my own, without seeking guidance from God, my spiritual GPS said, "REROUTING!"

I can laugh about it now because I'm glad I made that U-turn and returned to Him. Don't be distracted by distractions. That is a battle that goes on between your mind and heart. You want to do the right things (heart), but you also want to do what you want to do (mind). Choose to follow your heart.

I know you are grieving or experiencing hard times, but it doesn't mean your emotions will go away. However, everything is better with God. In the end, we are still human, and we will experience every emotion possible.

It has been years since the accident. There are still times when I think about my family and I get sad. I may weep, but I do not allow myself to stay in that place. If you stay somewhere too long, you may get stuck. I don't want to spend the rest of my life depressed and unhappy. I'm pretty sure your family members don't want you to do it either.

Decide, this day, that you will not allow yourself to get sad and slide into depression. You will live the life God has for you and live it abundantly. I'm a firm believer that if God brings you to it, He will see you through it.

Live!

He has a plan for us. I don't know about you, but in 2016, I decided to LIVE! Yes, it has been challenging, but I will not forfeit the promise. I'm standing on the Word of God and I'm going after everything He has for me. At the end of the day, it's all for His glory! Don't think about your next move; declare and decree today that you will LIVE!

I want to encourage you to walk by faith and trust God. Moving forward will be challenging, but it'll be worth it. It is necessary. My grandmother used to tell me all the time, "As long as you do your part, the rest will fall in place, and you'll get stars in your crown!" I remember that and have lived by it for over 12 years.

When you do what's right, God is pleased. When you step into flesh, God is not pleased. Push through the pain of all the hurt, disappointment, and betrayal, and move forward.

God is still there and He's on your side. I've realized that *I'm a chosen generation, a royal priesthood, a holy nation, His own special people, that will proclaim the praises of Him who called me out of darkness into His marvelous light*, as stated in 1 Peter 2:9 (NKJV). This is very cliché, but if God brings you to it, He will bring you through it.

Today is your day! You are free! You are healed! You are delivered! No longer will you be bothered with stress and heartache! No more fear! No more worries! Today is your day of victory! I'm decreeing that you will step out on faith and do what God has ordained you to do. Welcome to NEW life! Stay encouraged! Liiiiiiiiive!

Points to Ponder

1 - What is God speaking or telling you to do, but you're afraid to do it?

_____

_____

_____

2 - Moving forward, what are some things (or people) that you need to let go of or forgive?

_____

_____

_____

3 - Are you ready to LIVE?

_____

_____

_____

Meditation

Prayer

Father, I thank You for the opportunity to be able to share my story with others around the world. I pray that whatever is holding them in bondage, they will be loosed and freed from it on this very day! Touch and heal as only You can. Remove the doubt, fear, anxiety, and depression that they may be experiencing to cause them to miss You.

Free their minds and their hearts so that they can live for You from a pure place. Restore their minds! Give them the peace that surpasses all understanding. Give them knowledge, wisdom, and understanding to know that You make no mistakes and that You are God.

Heal their hearts so that they can be there for their children and family, but most importantly, for themselves. Touch the families as well. Let them know that You are in charge! Open their ear gates to hear positive things and receive from You.

Lord, if anyone isn't saved, I pray they have accepted You into their life! I pray they will know and realize that it is impossible to go through things and not have You on their side.

Heal, as only You can! Deliver, as only You can! Set free, as only You can, and we will give You the glory for it. We are thanking and praising You in advance because they are healed and set free! We believe it is already done in Jesus's name, AMEN

About the Author

When you feel your only hope is dying, but God comes and speaks a word and tells you to, "LIVE," you hold to those words for life!

My name is Arletha Orr. I know firsthand what it feels like to mentally die and be resurrected with Christ. A traumatic event happened in my life, and I know God is operating through me to help others. I'm just a lady from the country in the state of Mississippi who enjoys worshipping God, traveling, and serving others.

I'm an author who will take you on a journey of how God brought me through the toughest times in my life to victory. I'm a minister and certified life coach. My goal in life is to help others, live a life pleasing unto God, and help save souls for His Kingdom. It's not about me, but it's about rescuing people for God's Kingdom!

– Stay Connected –

Email: hello@arlethaorr.com
Website: www.arlethaorr.com
Facebook: Author Arletha Orr
Instagram: @arlethaorr

www.ingramcontent.com/pod-product-compliance
Lightning Source LLC
Chambersburg PA
CBHW050045120526
44589CB00038B/2737